Bugs in My Yard

LADYBUGS

Kim Thompson

TABLE OF CONTENTS

A Pelican Book

SEAHORSE PUBLISHING

Teaching Tips for Caregivers and Teachers:

Research shows that one of the best ways for students to learn a new topic is to read about it.

Before Reading

- Read the title and predict what the book will be about.
- Read the "Words to Know" and discuss the meaning of each word.
- Read the back cover to see what the book is about.

During Reading

- When a student gets to a word that is unknown, ask them to look at the rest of the sentence to find clues to help with the meaning of the unknown word.
- Motivate students with praise and encouragement.

After Reading

- Discuss the main idea of the book.
- Ask students to give one detail that they learned in the book.

Sight Words

a
away
can
eat
find
fly
have
little
many
on
what
you

Words to Know

aphids

colors

ladybug

leaf

spots

What can you find on a **leaf**?

leaf

You can find a little **ladybug**!

ladybug

Ladybugs have many **colors**.

colors

Ladybugs can have **spots**.

spots

Ladybugs eat **aphids**.

aphids

A ladybug can fly away!

Index

Written by: Kim Thompson
Design by: Under the Oaks Media
Series Development: James Earley

Photos: Kotoimages: cover; Carlos Caetano: p. 5; Dr Foto: p. 7; Dr.alex_Dreamstime: p. 8-9; Be Good: p. 11; Victoria M Gardner: p. 13; poidl: p. 14-15

Library of Congress PCN Data
Ladybugs / Kim Thompson
Bugs in My Yard
ISBN 978-1-63897-427-7(hard cover)
ISBN 978-1-63897-542-7(paperback)
ISBN 978-1-63897-657-8(EPUB)
ISBN 978-1-63897-772-8(eBook)
Library of Congress Control Number: 2021953293

Printed in Canada/102024/CP20241007

Seahorse Publishing Company
www.seahorsepub.com

Published in the United States
Seahorse Publishing
PO Box 771325
Coral Springs, FL 33077

SEAHORSE PUBLISHING